AVAILABLE NOW
from Lerner Publishing Services!

The *On the Hardwood* series:

Atlanta Hawks	Los Angeles Lakers
Boston Celtics	Memphis Grizzlies
Brooklyn Nets	Miami Heat
Chicago Bulls	Minnesota Timberwolves
Cleveland Cavaliers	New York Knicks
Dallas Mavericks	Oklahoma City Thunder
Denver Nuggets	Phoenix Suns
Detroit Pistons	Philadelphia 76ers
Golden State Warriors	Portland Trail Blazers
Houston Rockets	San Antonio Spurs
Indiana Pacers	Utah Jazz
Los Angeles Clippers	Washington Wizards

Hoop City   Long Shot

Basketball fans: *don't miss these hoops books from MVP's wing-man, Scobre Educational.*

These titles, and many others, are available at www.scobre.com.

Lerner™

To Order • www.lernerbooks.com • 800-328-4929 • fax 800-332-1132

ON THE HARDWOOD

WIZARDS

BEN MISH

On the Hardwood: Washington Wizards

MVP Books
2255 Calle Clara
La Jolla, CA 92037

MVP Books is an imprint of Scobre Educational, a division of Book Buddy Digital Media, Inc.,
42982 Osgood Road, Fremont, CA 94539

MVP Books publications may be purchased for
educational, business, or sales promotional use.

Cover and layout design by Jana Ramsay
Copyedited by Susan Sylvia
Photos by Getty Images

ISBN: 978-1-61570-926-7 (Library Binding)
ISBN: 978-1-61570-925-0 (Soft Cover)

TABLE OF CONTENTS

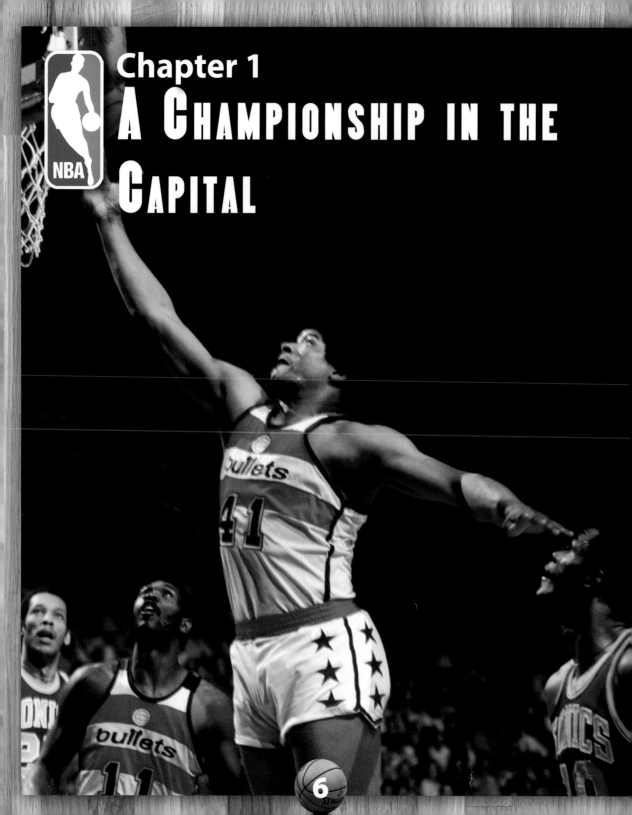

Chapter 1
A CHAMPIONSHIP IN THE CAPITAL

When we think about our nation's capital, the halls of Congress and the bustle of politicians immediately come to mind. Tokens from American history, like the Lincoln Memorial and the Washington Monument, make up Washington D.C.'s unique cityscape. However, politics is not the only high-powered game in the city.

Venture to the Verizon Center and you will see pieces of basketball history all around. Proudly hanging are four retired numbers of basketball greats: Earl Monroe (10), Elvin Hayes (11), Gus Johnson (25), and Wes Unseld (41). Watch basketball games on TV and you will hear announcers

Earl the Pearl

Earl Monroe was known for his flashy dribbling, passing, and play-making, which kept opponents off guard. He was also called "Thomas Edison" as a kid by his friends for making up new and unusual moves on the court.

like Steve Buckhantz and Phil Chenier bring those hardwood battles to life. You can also read about the Washington Wizards in the *Washington Post*—the capital's

The Lincoln Memorial in Washington, D.C.

oldest newspaper—as writers connect the franchise's storied past to its current season.

The tradition of basketball in D.C. is actually much bigger than the team's retired numbers or its win-loss record. D.C.'s community has truly embraced the game. There are a ton of programs for kids in schools that allow them to develop their skills at an early age. Many players from the D.C. area, superstar Kevin Durant included, have gone on to become high school and college All-Americans. Their development was originally nurtured by these schoolyard programs. One might say that, for its size, D.C. has done more than any urban area in furthering the sport.

Therefore, it is surprising to learn that Washington, D.C. did not always have a professional basketball team. The story of the Washington Wizards actually began in Chicago in 1961. At that time, the team was known as the Chicago Packers—named for the city's meat

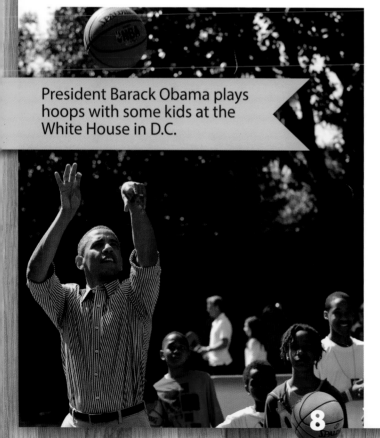

President Barack Obama plays hoops with some kids at the White House in D.C.

packing district. The Packers had a very rough start during their first season, and finished in last place with a record of 18-62. There was, however, a bright spot during this shaky beginning. Walt Bellamy—their first round draft pick in 1961—was

Bellamy was inducted into the Basketball Hall of Fame in 1993, then again in 2010 with the 1960 Olympic Basketball Team.

an awesome talent, and his Rookie of the Year award proved as much. In his first year, Bellamy was the league's second leading scorer with an average of 31.6 points per game.

The next year the team changed their name to the Zephyrs—possibly because they wanted a fresh start after their terrible first season. "Zephyr" is the name of the Greek God of the West Wind, and is also the name of a famous train from Chicago. However, the new name didn't do much to change the team's luck. The Chicago-based team finished in last place again with a 25-55 record. However, the Zephyrs

Olympian Joins the Team
Walt Bellamy played in the 1960 Summer Olympics in Rome, Italy, where the team went undefeated and won a gold medal.

did have another promising player on their team. Terry Dischinger, who was a member of the 1960 USA Men's Olympic Basketball Team, won the 1962-63 Rookie of the Year award.

The city of Chicago was ready to rally around their fledgling franchise—especially after players from their team snagged the Rookie of the Year award in consecutive seasons. However, before Chicago could really embrace their team, the winds of change blew for the Zephyrs. The team moved to Baltimore the following season, where they became the Baltimore Bullets. Their third name seemed to be the charm, and the Bullets finished a much improved 4th place in the Western Division.

In 1964-65, the Baltimore Bullets advanced to the playoffs for the first time in franchise history. The Bullets beat the St. Louis Hawks and went to the Western Conference Finals, where they unfortunately lost to the L.A. Lakers. When they followed this up by advancing to the

Terry Dischinger poses in 1963. As a member of the Chicago Zephyrs, he won the NBA Rookie of the Year award.

Conference Semifinals the next season, it became clear that the young team was poised to become a real contender in the NBA. However, to become champions, the Bullets needed an extra push—a star who could bring the team together and lead them to greatness. Luckily, a player named Wes Unseld was on the way.

Following his stint as an All-American at Louisville, Unseld was chosen by the Baltimore Bullets as the #2 pick overall in the 1968 NBA Draft. People immediately took notice. During his first year, Unseld won both the Rookie of the Year and Most Valuable Player awards. Unseld was only the second player in the history of the NBA to receive both of these honors in the same season.

Unseld was called "The Wall" because he was difficult to navigate around, and he soon became infamous for setting bone-crushing screens. Unseld did not possess exceptional height. His listed height was 6'7" (and he admitted at retirement he was actually only 6'6")—but he

Wes Unseld, shown in 1970, was an intimidating force on the basketball court.

Wes Unseld had a competitive rivalry with Milwaukee's Kareem Abdul Jabbar during the 1971 NBA Finals.

times. In 1981, Wes Unseld's number 41 jersey was retired by the team, never to be worn again. Unlike many of his peers, who moved from team to team, Unseld spent all of his years with the Bullets. The center/power forward played almost 1,000 games for the same franchise.

played with great force on the court.

Throughout his career, the Louisville, Kentucky, native rebounded exceptionally well, set wicked picks, and ignited fast-breaks with his passes up the court. He led the Bullets to the NBA Finals four

The Bullets' All-Star

During his 13 seasons with the Bullets, Wes Unseld was selected for five All-Star teams.

Unseld became the Bullets' undeniable leader and, as the 1970s progressed, the Bullets were a success. The Bullets made it all the way to the NBA Finals in 1971, where they faced the Milwaukee Bucks. Unfortunately, Milwaukee's star duo of Kareem Abdul-Jabbar and Oscar Robertson overpowered the Bullets. Those Future Hall of Famers may have denied Unseld and his team a championship banner, but just reaching the NBA Finals was a huge accomplishment. Baltimore fans were thrilled for their team, and looked forward to more stellar seasons to come.

As the 1970s continued, it became clear the Bullets were just a breath away from becoming NBA champions. They had a lot of success in the playoffs—including another trip to the NBA Finals in 1975—but always seemed to fall just short of greatness.

The Bullets also had another huge change during this time period. In 1973, the team moved to a suburb of Washington D.C., where they eventually became

The Washington Monument stands tall in D.C.'s skyline.

What's in a Name?
Before they were the Washington Bullets, the team was called the Capital Bullets for one season.

the Washington Bullets. D.C. fans were thrilled to have a professional basketball team, and attendance rose drastically: from 263,660 in 1972-73, to 414,202 in 1973-74. The team boasted the 5th highest attendance in the league that season.

Then, in 1977-78, all of the pieces suddenly came together. The Washington Bullets had a huge star in Wes Unseld, and a deep, talented roster. They also had a new coach, Dick Motta, who had joined the team just a year earlier. Though Motta had never won an NBA Championship, he took home the 1971 NBA Coach of the Year award while coaching the Chicago Bulls. When he left Chicago for Washington, Motta had an NBA Championship in his sights.

In 1977-78, the Bullets advanced to the NBA Finals, where they took on the

Coach Dick Motta was an award-winning coach for Chicago before he came to D.C.

14

Seattle SuperSonics. After a grueling, seven-game series, the Bullets emerged victorious. After 17 years as a franchise, they were finally champions. Wes Unseld added to his list of growing honors when he was named MVP of the NBA Finals.

The people of Washington, D.C. were ecstatic. The Bullets' victory was truly the crowning moment in a remarkably successful period for the franchise. The city's team had accomplished amazing things—collecting six division titles, four conference titles, and an NBA Championship during the 1960s and 1970s. As the 1970s came to a close, Unseld's playing career also wound down, and he eventually retired in

Wes Unseld stretches for a rebound against the SuperSonics in the 1978 NBA finals.

1981. Wes Unseld's greatness did not go unnoticed, and he was inducted into the Basketball Hall of Fame in 1988. Not only does Unseld's retired number hang in the Verizon Center, but in 1996, he was named one of the 50 greatest players in NBA history.

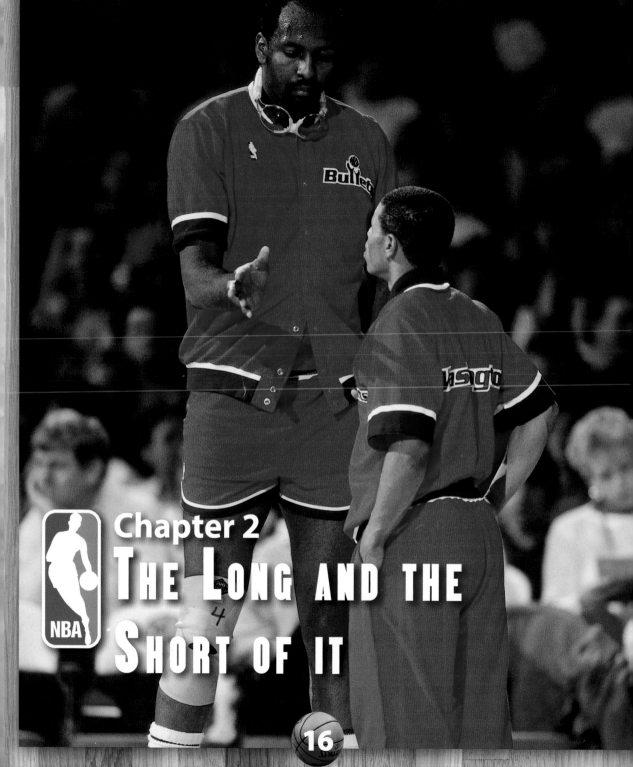

Chapter 2
The Long and the Short of It

The 1970s Bullets teams were simply incredible. They were a constant presence in the playoffs, and they made Washington D.C. stand for more than politics and historical monuments. For a few glorious seasons, it felt like D.C. was also the basketball capital of America. At the beginning of the 1980s, however, there was a slight change. By 1981, things had declined to the point that the Bullets were out of the playoff picture entirely. For the first time in 12 years, the playoffs would begin without the team from D.C.

Though the Bullets did recover in time to make it back to the playoffs during the following

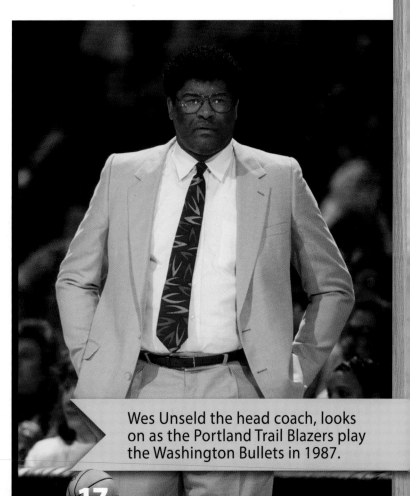

Wes Unseld the head coach, looks on as the Portland Trail Blazers play the Washington Bullets in 1987.

seasons, first round exits became common. It looked like the glory days of the 1970s were truly over. What caused the sudden dip? Some of the decline could be attributed to age, as players retired and moved on. Other issues were due to injuries. Sometimes, good fortune just runs out.

Scanning the Bullets' stats for the 1980s, you would not see an amazing win-loss record. But any Washington fan could tell you that there were still many memorable moments during that decade. One player who brought some magic to the team during theose rather average years was Manute Bol. He came from the extreme poverty of the Sudan in Africa to join the team in 1985. At 7'7", Bol was the tallest

Manute Bol used his incredible length to swat over 2,000 shots in his 10 year NBA career.

player in the league. This talented center also set the record for most blocked shots per game in the 1985-86 season. However, statistics alone did not propel his team to victory, and the Bullets finished the season with a losing record. Bol's presence, however, provided a much needed slice of excitement for the team's fans.

Muggsy Bogues drives to the basket in a game during his years at Wake Forest University.

Bol would have stood out from a crowd no matter what. But, when a new teammate was drafted in 1987, Bol suddenly looked like a true giant. This new player was Muggsy Bogues. Before he put on the Bullets' jersey, Bogues had been a star player at Wake Forest University in North Carolina. Yet despite his tremendous skill, he was mostly recognized as

Cover Guys

The fact that Bogues was the shortest and Bol was the tallest player in the history of the NBA was a big story, attracting much attention. The duo was on the cover of three magazines in 1987-88.

the shortest player in NBA history – standing just 5'3" tall. When Bol and Bogues stood side by side, Bogues only came up to his teammate's waist! By the time he retired, however, Bogues had proven that he wasn't some sideshow. In fact, he was 16th on the NBA's all-time assist list.

The 1980s marked not only a tough time for the Bullets, but for the city that housed the team. Though there were pockets of wealth in the nation's capital, the streets of D.C. told a different story. Crime began to overtake the poorer areas of D.C. During this time, the city established inner city basketball leagues. For those in the community who wanted to get off of D.C.'s streets, these leagues offered kids a chance to play ball, and get out of harm's way.

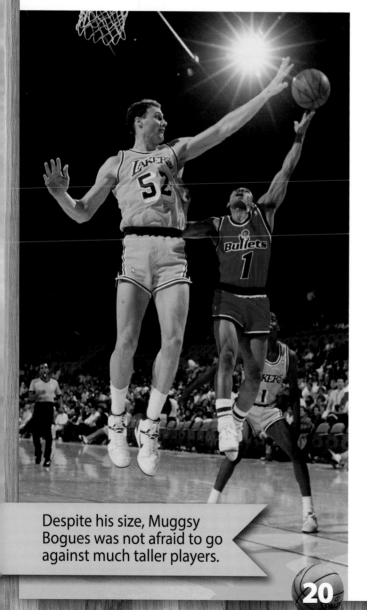

Despite his size, Muggsy Bogues was not afraid to go against much taller players.

Kids play a pick-up game of basketball, a hugely popular pastime in Washington, D.C.

In his autobiography, *In the Land of Giants: My Life in Basketball,* Muggsy Bogues wrote about the struggles of growing up poor in inner city Baltimore. His early challenges, however, only made him work harder for his dreams. Muggsy Bogues became an inspiration to many of the inner city kids in the D.C. area.

Another player who was a huge boost to fan morale during the 1980s was NBA star Moses Malone. Malone was traded from the 76ers

Street Ball Matchup

Street ball has been a longtime tradition in D.C. Legend has it that as far back as 1957, Wilt Chamberlain and Elgin Baylor faced off in a series of street ball matches on Washington, D.C. playgrounds.

stints with the Rockets and the 76ers. In fact, while playing with Philadelphia, he broke a record against Washington—racking up 15 offensive rebounds in a single game.

In his first year with the Bullets, Malone not only averaged an impressive 24.1 points per game, but he further proved his worth when he was selected for the 1987 All-Star Team. Though Malone only played for the Bullets for a short time—from 1986 to 1988—he was a central

to the Bullets in 1986. Prior to his arrival in Washington, many Bullets fans remembered Malone well for

part of those Washington teams. He even scored his 20,000th point while wearing a Bullets' jersey. In 1986-87,

Malone also scored 50 points in a game, becoming one of only three Bullets ever to do so. Malone will always be remembered as one of the greatest players to play for the Bullets. In retirement, Moses Malone was named one of the NBA's 50 Greatest Players.

Despite Malone's presence during the 1980s, playoff victories were fewer and further between. But a quick glance up to the rafters at the Verizon Center reminded fans of what was once good, and soon could be again.

Moses Malone salutes the crowd, the year he was inducted into the Hall of Fame.

Chapter 3
BRING ON THE WIZARDS

As the Washington Bullets ventured into the 1990s, the team was a bit weary from the ups and downs of the 1980s. The 1990s represented a new beginning, and a new face helped to kick-start a fresh decade. The Bullets broke new ground off the court by hiring Susan O'Malley as the president of their organization. O'Malley made history when she became the first female team president in NBA history. Despite this achievement, the 1990s proved to be a difficult decade for the franchise. Though the Bullets used to be frequent postseason visitors, they only

Pass the Puck
Susan O'Malley's father, Peter O'Malley, was formerly the president of Washington, D.C.'s professional hockey team, the Washington Capitals.

advanced to the playoffs once during the 1990s.

It could be said that sports is a barometer of the overall mood of a society. During the early 1990s, the lukewarm mood of the fans

Susan O'Malley became a strong female voice in a male-dominated sport when she became president of the Wizards.

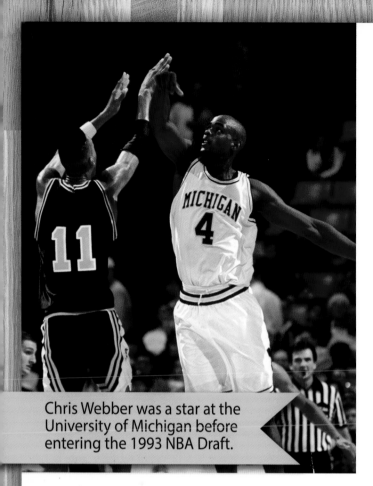

Chris Webber was a star at the University of Michigan before entering the 1993 NBA Draft.

friends, community members, and fans from the entire region. Sports can give fans a shot of energy. Sports can also provide them with a meaningful routine, and allow a large group of people to root for a common cause.

Fans tend to look for one main thing in a great basketball team: a leader. During the 1990s, the team and the city both looked to one player to fill this role: 6' 10" power forward Chris Webber. Webber had been a high school star in Michigan before playing college ball at the University of Michigan. In college, Webber was part of a group of young and trend-setting players who were nicknamed the "Fab Five."

in Washington, D.C. was due in part to the average play of their team on the basketball court. It is hard to rally behind a losing team. When the home team is winning, it is a point of pride for their fans. The basketball games in sold-out arenas become a meeting spot for

With his posse, Webber twice led the University of Michigan to the NCAA Finals. After such a successful college career, Webber was then the first overall pick in the 1993 NBA Draft. When he was traded the to Bullets in 1994, many fans believed in Webber, and were convinced that he was the right guy to lead their franchise back to the playoffs.

Webber's tenure in D.C. started out strong—he averaged 20.9 points per game in 1994-95. However, the very next year, injuries plagued "C-Webb." He was only able to play 15 games during the entire 1995-96 season. Fans were discouraged, and thought

that Webber's injuries were more of the same bad luck that had seemed to follow their team. However, when the 6'10" power forward regained his health the next season, he

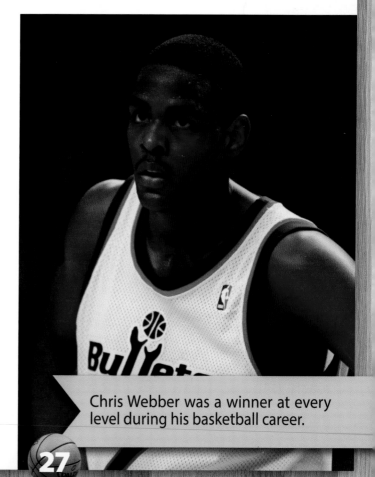

Chris Webber was a winner at every level during his basketball career.

27

Chris Webber's hustle and leadership carried the team to the playoffs for the first time in nine years.

Though the Bullets lost to the Chicago Bulls in the first round of the playoffs, there was a lot of excitement that spring. With their new star—Chris Webber—on board and healthy, fans were certain that things were going to turn around.

Along with this new hope for their team's future came a desire to move forward with a new nickname. Many people thought that the longstanding team name, the Bullets, was no longer appropriate for the city they loved.

Due to the intense violence and crime around Washington, the name "Bullets" came to represent everything that basketball didn't

immediately carved out his niche as the team's next big thing. Webber not only was the second leading scorer on the team (forward Juwan Howard scored the most points that season), but he also helped lead the team to the 1997 playoffs. This was the first time that the Bullets had reached the postseason in almost a decade.

want to be. Basketball was supposed to be a break from real problems, not a constant reminder of them. The team's old slogan, "Faster than a speeding bullet," no longer felt like a fun phrase. This all added up to one verdict: the name "Bullets" had to go. The organization decided they would hold a contest to choose a

new, more positive team name. More than 2,000 dif-ferent nicknames were entered in the contest, with the top five being the Dragons, the Express, the Sea Dogs, the Stallions, and the

The players fought hard on the court to turn the newly-named Wizards into a winning team.

Owner Abe Pollin engaged the community by holding a contest to come up with a new team name.

tongue. Though some people were thrilled with the new name, many fans did not like the change, because the Bullets had been such a huge part of their lives. It was hard to let a piece of their city's history go. This was, after all, one of the only times in NBA history that a team had changed its name and rebranded itself without moving to a different location. The only other time this had happened was when the Chicago Packers changed to the Chicago Zephryrs in 1962.

Wizards.

Finally, after fans were asked to vote from these top five choices, the Washington Wizards emerged as the winner. This new name was alliterative, like "The Baltimore Bullets" had been—meaning that each word started with the same letter—and easily rolled off the

In 1997, the Wizards moved into their current home arena, now known as the Verizon Center. The arena is also home to the

The Wizards played the SuperSonics in December of 1997 for the team's first game in the new arena. President Bill Clinton was in attendance.

Georgetown Hoyas, a storied college basketball program. With their new home court, new nickname and logo—a wizard in a long blue robe, holding a basketball—the Washington Wizards and their fans were hopeful. They wanted to show the world that their team, and their city, could rise above the past and build towards a fantastic future. The

city didn't know it yet, but another big change was heading their way—in the form of the GOAT, the "Greatest Player of All Time."

Go Hoyas!

Georgetown University has produced famous world leaders like former President Bill Clinton. The men's basketball team is also known for producing great talent. Patrick Ewing, Dikembe Mutombo, and Allen Iverson are all Georgetown alumni.

Chapter 4
CONTENDERS IN THE NEW MILLENNIUM

All-Stars, MVPs, and Rookie of the Year Award winners have all played in Washington over the years. In 2000, the man some consider to be the greatest player to ever play the game, Michael Jordan, became affiliated with the team. After many years with the Chicago Bulls, Jordan retired. But he was itching to get back into basketball, and joined Washington as the president of basketball operations. He was also an owner with a minority share of the Wizards. For the first time since their 1970's glory days, all eyes were truly on the Washington team. The country couldn't wait to see what the famous Michael Jordan would accomplish with his newest franchise.

Soon after his arrival, the 6'6" shooting guard moved from the back offices to the actual basketball court. Jordan was 38 years old, and slower than he had been in his prime, but he wanted one last shot at the glory of an NBA Championship. By trading his suit for a uniform, Jordan was forced to sell his ownership

Michael Jordan first joined the Wizards in the back offices as President of Basketball Operations.

share of the Wizards. Being an owner and a player simultaneously worked against the NBA's policy.

Michael Jordan brought his superstar status to the Wizards as he elevated the team on the court and off.

Jordan started strong, and was a valuable mentor for the younger Wizards. Unfortunately, a knee injury derailed some of his 2001-02 campaign with the team. But the 10-time NBA scoring champion returned for the 2002-03 season, and he played well. Victories were still difficult to come by, yet Jordan was a fearless competitor, and he led others by example.

The Brooklyn-born Jordan breathed new life into the organization, bringing his first-rate play and attitude to the squad. Fans flocked to fill the arena, and attendance jumped by more than 200,000 (a 31.5 % increase) during the 2001-02 season—propelling D.C.

Michael Jordan waves goodbye before his last career game against the Philadelphia 76ers on April 16, 2003.

from 18th to 3rd in NBA attendance. Jordan also brought a new level of desirability to the Wizards, as fans across the country tuned in to see how an all-time great was fairing after coming back from his second retirement.

Even though Jordan had enough enthusiasm for the game to fill up an entire arena, after a few years in D.C., he was starting to feel his age. He knew that his playing days were limited. Before he left the team after the

Welcome Back!

Jordan retired from the Chicago Bulls in 1993 to pursue a career in baseball. Then, he returned to the Bulls in 1995. After snagging a few more championships, MJ retired for a second time in 1999.

Antawn Jamison proudly holds his new Wizards jersey.

was labeled "40 at 40." When Jordan played his last game in April 2003, the fans gave him a three minute standing ovation.

After Jordan entered his third and final retirement from professional basketball, a few key cogs in the Wizards' machine soon emerged. Their names: Antawn Jamison, Larry Hughes, and Gilbert Arenas. During the 2004-05 regular season, the three Wizards combined to score more points than any other trio in the league.

Jamison was well-regarded for his scoring ability and durability. His career scoring average of 18.8 points per game and his sixteen (and counting) years in the league attest to as much. Hughes was a

2002-03 season, Jordan did manage a few impressive accomplishments— not just for a player his age, but for any player. During a 2003 game, Jordan scored 43 points—a feat that

pest, well-thought-of defensively, due to his fast hands and ability to step in opponents' passing lanes. He led the NBA in steals during the 2004-05 season. Arenas was known as both "Agent Zero" and "Hibachi" because of his ability to quickly heat up and lead the Wizards to victory.

The trio of Jamison, Hughes, and Arenas steered the Wizards to the playoffs. The 2004-05 season will be remembered as the time when the franchise happily disposed of some very long-standing streaks. First, the team enjoyed their best regular season in 26 years, posting a 45-37 record. Beyond that, the team also reached the postseason for the first time as the Washington Wizards. When the team reached the playoffs, Washington achieved another

milestone and snapped another ugly streak. In the opening round of the NBA Playoffs, the Wizards defeated

Larry Hughes elevates during a 2004 game against the Miami Heat.

37

Chinese Connection

After leaving the NBA, Gilbert Arenas played for the Shanghai Sharks in the Chinese Basketball Association.

the Chicago Bulls in six games, thereby becoming only the 12th team in NBA history to rally to win a playoff series after losing the first two games. The Game 6 victory also marked the franchise's first playoff series win in 23

Gilbert Arenas and LeBron James square off in a post-season game. Their playoff rivalry persisted for three straight years.

years. Shortly thereafter, the Miami Heat swept the Wizards out of the playoffs, but that didn't detract from a season well spent.

In 2006, the Wizards also reached the playoffs. Once there, they were greeted by the Cleveland Cavaliers and their emerging superstar, LeBron James. The virtually even series eventually went in Cleveland's direction as James outlasted Arenas. This series ignited three straight years of playoff matchups between the Wizards and Cavaliers.

Despite losing to Cleveland in 2006, Arenas' play catapulted him into one of the game's elite and he earned a six-year max contract. Unfortunately for Arenas and the Wizards, he wasn't able to fulfill the promise of that deal due to a series of injuries during the span of the contract.

As Washington and their fans looked to the future, they knew that they needed some young talent to bridge the gap between themselves and the top of the Eastern Conference. The Wizards also needed to stay healthy. Injuries dotted the first decade of the 21st century and prevented the team from reaching its ultimate goal of an NBA Championship. At some point, even a Wizard simply had to hope for better luck.

Wizards fans cheer for their team during a 2008 playoff game against Cleveland.

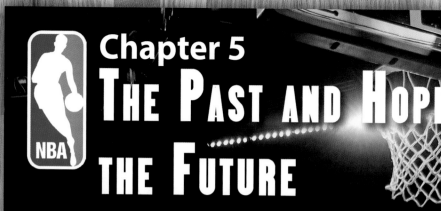

Chapter 5
THE PAST AND HOPE FOR THE FUTURE

The story of the NBA draft can be a frustrating one. So much about the draft is simply up to luck. Sometimes the best players are not the top draft picks. Sometimes the top draft picks get injured. It is hard to know if a top pick will ever deliver for their team.

In 2010, the Wizards' luck changed for the better, and they won the NBA lottery. Using their top pick, Washington selected lightning-quick point guard John Wall. Wall, who was born and raised in North Carolina, played college ball for the University of Kentucky before he was drafted by the Wizards. The spotlight shone bright at the University of Kentucky, where Coach John Calipari turned out first-round picks on a yearly basis. So, Wall wasn't easily intimidated when he joined the pro ranks.

The 6′ 4″, 195-pound point guard started off strong in the NBA. In only his third professional game, Wall had nine steals—tying a Washington

John Wall prepares to shoot a free throw.

Wizards fans get fired up before a game against the Cleveland Cavaliers at the Verizon Center.

franchise record. Wall also recorded a triple double during his rookie season with 19 points, 13 assists, and 10 rebounds, becoming one of the youngest NBA players to accomplish such a feat.

Wall played in the 2011 Rookie Game during All-Star Weekend and was named MVP of the contest. That season, he just missed another more important honor as Blake Griffin took home the Rookie of the Year award, while Wall finished 2nd in the voting. Due to a knee injury, Wall had to wait to get his 2012-13 season on track. When he came back and started to work his magic, fans were elated. Once Wall was healthy, he dazzled his home fans and provided hope for the future. By working with his frontcourt mates, Nenê and Emeka Okafor, Wall consistently provided stellar play both as a distributor and a scorer. On March 25, 2013, everything came together for Wall on the offensive end as he poured in a career-high 47 points against the Memphis Grizzlies.

Thankfully for Wizards' fans, Wall is not going anyplace anytime soon. In the summer of 2013, Wall signed a five year, $80 million contract extension. Thus, the Wizards' backcourt will be in good hands for many years to come. Point guard, Wall, and shooting guard, Bradley Beal, have formed a strong partnership. Beal, who played his college ball at the University of Florida, is 20 years old and was drafted third overall in the 2012 draft. These two young players will also benefit from the veteran

From left to right: Head Coach Randy Wittman, team owner Ted Leonsis, John Wall, and general manager Ernie Grunfeld, announced a new contract for Wall on August 1, 2013.

A Valued Player

When Nenê returned from his cancer scare in 2008, the fans gave him a standing ovation. He went on to lead the league in field goal percentage during the 2010-11 season.

players on the roster, and all of the experience they bring to the Wizards.

Bradley Beal shoots against the Indiana Pacers during a 2012 game.

One of the veteran players that Wall and Beal can lean on is Nenê. He came to the team in March 2012, and brought with him over a decade of experience as a professional basketball player. A native of Brazil, he was born Maybyner Rodney Hilário, but is known as Nenê, which means "baby" in his native language. He received the name as a child because he was the youngest in his family.

Nenê led the Brazilian National team in the 2001 Goodwill Games before being drafted in the first round of the 2002 NBA Draft. In 10 seasons with the Nuggets, he led Denver in career field goal percentage. After this promising start, however, Nenê had a medical scare that could have ended his NBA career. In January, 2008, Nenê was diagnosed with cancer, and was absent from the NBA for three months after having a small tumor removed. When he returned in March, 2008, Nenê posted his best season ever, and became a fan favorite in Denver. The 6'11" power forward/center has tremendous rebounding ability, versatility, and leadership skills—all of which makes him a great asset to the Wizards.

Wall and Beal are promising young talents, yet they will need to buck recent Wizards' history to stay healthy and on the floor. Once these two players are on the court together and consistently performing well, the duo should return the Wizards to the glory days of the 1970s. The duo won't have

Nenê gets ready to shoot against the New York Knicks at Madison Square Garden in New York.

Otto Porter points to the crowd with excitement after being picked # 3 overall by the Washington Wizards in the 2013 NBA Draft.

With the third pick in the 2013 NBA draft, the Wizards stayed local and plucked Georgetown forward Otto Porter from the Hoyas. Porter will add to the core of young, highly drafted talent. For a town that loves its local and homegrown heroes, Porter will receive extra support from the fans at the Verizon Center—the very same fans that also supported him in college.

Ownership will also play a big role in the ongoing Wizards rebuilding efforts. Since he bought the Wizards in 2010, new owner Ted Leonsis has shown that he

to do it alone. Beyond Nenê, Beal, and sharp-shooter, Trevor Ariza, the Wizards added another piece in the 2013 draft.

Family Tradition

Otto Porter's dad, Otto Porter, Sr., holds the high school record at Missouri's Scott County Central High School for rebounds at 1,733. His mother, Elnora Porter, also went to SCC, and was an all-state basketball player in 1985.

cares what the fans think, and has made himself accessible to his team's supporters. Wizards' fans can connect with him via email and on his web site. The team owner has also written a manifesto of all the things he wants to do to transform the Wizards into a championship team. One of the steps Leonsis made was to shift the team's colors back to the red, white, and blue of the 1970's Bullets, when wins were common.

The full rebuild of the Washington Wizards is almost complete. The team is moving forward in the right direction with a talented young roster. With the dynamic duo of Wall and Beal, along with the inside strength from a veteran like Nenê, the franchise has a chance to be a real contender in the coming years. The future is bright for the Washington Wizards.

Bradley Beal, Nenê, and John Wall pose for a team picture. They are poised to lead the team to a bright future.

Wizards fans cheer the team on at Verizon Center.